FIND YOUR AUTHENTIC VOICE™

The courage to express who you truly are.

Your greatest ally is born when you courageously speak your truth and claim your unique power.

FIND YOUR AUTHENTIC VOICE COPYRIGHT

Copyright © 2010-2013 by Miranda J. Barrett.
Original Concept Copyright © 2008 by Miranda J. Barrett.
Copyright © 2010 Front Cover Artwork by Helena Nelson-Reed.

All rights reserved. This book may not be reproduced in whole or in part without written permission. In accordance with the U.S. Copyright act of 1976, the scanning, uploading and electronic sharing of any part of this book without permission of the publisher is unlawful piracy and theft of the author's intellectual property.

If you would like to use material from the book (other than for review purposes), prior written permission must be obtained by contacting either the publisher at:

Info@MirandaJBarrett.com
or the artist at www.HelenaNelsonReed.com
Thank you for the support of the author and the artist's rights.

please note:

The written or spoken information, ideas, procedures and suggestions contained and presented in 'FIND YOUR AUTHENTIC VOICE' workshops and books are meant for educational purposes only and are not for diagnosis. It should not be used as a substitute for your physician's advice. 'FIND YOUR AUTHENTIC VOICE' is not therapy and is not intended to replace the recommendations of a licensed health practitioner. It is the responsibility of the reader to consult with their own medical Doctor, Counselor, Therapist or other competent professional regarding any condition before adopting any of the suggestions in this book.

FIND YOUR AUTHENTIC VOICE™

Dedicated to the true essence which resides within us all and the conviction to express this unique sword of truth.

MISSION STATEMENT

To guide and facilitate women
in becoming their most beautiful and radiant selves.

To acknowledge and embrace the well of love
and power which lies within all women and to ignite the
awakening and embodying of this life force.

To empower each woman, through exquisite self-care and love,
to live her fullest life possible, and to walk her path of wisdom
and truth, as she shares this light and knowledge
with all beings.

IN DEEP GRATITUDE

Thank you

The creation, birth and life of 'A Woman's Truth' would not have been possible without the love, support and devotion from the following angels in my life:

My beautiful daughter Megan who naturally embodies the teachings of living in her truth and integrity, thank you for the creative gift of the beautiful artwork. Helena Nelson-Reed for her generosity of spirit in allowing her extraordinary artwork, which embodies the teachings so magnificently, to grace the covers. Dennise Marie Keller for her unwavering support and dedication to the teachings and for proofing, editing, aligning and translating my vision into the technical world of manifestation. Dan Fowler for his creative genius and dedication. Lucy Alexander and Suzanne Ryan, my dearest friends for their amazing editing and wholehearted encouragement. Monica Marsh for her commitment, support and belief in the workshops. Maggie Crawford, my mum, for her proofing and for being a living example of the teachings. Cait Myer and Katie Steen for their patience and ability to decipher my handwriting and for formatting the books. Bethany Kelly for her support. Deborah Waring for holding the space for the conception of 'A Woman's Truth' to be born and for her insight in the first year of teaching and Emmanuel for believing in my vision.

My mentors and teachers Rod Stryker, Adyashanti and Alison Armstrong, Max Simon and Jeffrey Van Dyk for their continuous and guiding light in my life, their never-ending belief in my potential and for always teaching me the way to evolve into my highest and most potent self. And to all of you beautiful and courageous women who are committing to living your truth and transforming into your most radiant selves,

thank you.

A PRELUDE

An overture to speaking your truth.

These words are some of the keys to the wisdom that resides within the covers of 'Finding your True Voice'. Within the context of spiritual guidebooks, Miranda Barrett has penned a text of insight and honesty. The subject of unveiling the truth about ourselves, for many, is a monumental intimidating task. With the keys, inquiries and guidelines Miranda imparts for women, finding your true voice is a guided formula for freedom.

The journey of our life here is an adventure that can fragment our spirits. Our 'stories', our 'traumas and dramas' become what we identify with. Even though they actually become our identities, they are not us, not our true selves. When we accept the mission to free our suppressed voice, Miranda has a set of keys that when applied and practiced, allows us to re - member our true selves by beginning to speak with our true voice. This freedom and transformation leads to feeling and being more fully self expressed in our daily lives.

This book is a journey into self-discovery and self-realization. In our regular lives, we play many roles that often obscure our true selves. When our true self is obscured, our true voice is obscured. Miranda has key steps that can lead you back to yourself. It is called a 'truth inquiry.'

As we travel through the steps and revelations of a 'truth inquiry', 'releasing secrets and lies', 'releasing shame and blame' and then 'learning how to listen', we arrive at our true selves and our true voices.

So in these auspicious times, why not set aside
your confining stories and suppressed voices?

Welcome yourselves to the new adventure of Finding Your True Voice!

~ Valdez Flagg
Chairman of the Screen Actors Guild
Stage Manager ~ Seeker of the Truth

In the spirit of authenticity and with a warm hug of gratefulness for this humbling invitation to be included in this wonderful book, here is my gift to you and your readers written from my heart.

Finding Me

Is this me?
The sabateur
Who holds back in that
One split second,
On the cusp of giving life
To what terrifies me to the bone
Harnesses my energy
Strangles my being
That daunting thought
Of sharing my opinion.

Oh my god.
The tension, the fear, the sweat
In that moment of decision
When the words have formed
And lined up in a sentence
Fenced in my mind's eye
Where the guardian of shame
Slams the door and says
Not now.

In a crushing blow to spontaneity
How I mourned the chance
To reveal a part of me
Dying to catch
The breath, the tone, the lyrics of my soul
And what could have been
A beautiful expression instead
Dissipates in silent embarrassment.

Only to be saved
By the loyal understudies of truth
Who thrive in playing the losing game of pleasing
Who so confidently take orders
From the people in the room
Who've arrived with their own menus
Who's agenda is
Me first, not you.

Is this me?
The impostor at the masquerade party
Who looks like me from the outside
How impersonates me flawlessly
Who pretends to be engaged and present in the moment
But who instead is wrestling behind wool curtains
Stained in the regret and irony of knowing
There is a me inside
That is uncompromisingly me
Who desperately wants to smuggle in
Any morsel of pureness
And stowaway to the cradle of authenticity
Where her unborn child can be rocked
Ever so gently to sleep.

~ **Pear Urushima**
Poet

FIND YOUR AUTHENTIC VOICE™
Gems of Love

FINDING YOUR TRUE VOICE 1

BROUGHT TO THE LIGHT 4

BECOMING A TRUTH TELLER 5

OBSTACLES TO LIVING YOUR TRUTH 8

SPEAKING YOUR TRUTH INQUIRY 14

SECRETS AND LIES 18

SPEAKING THE TRUTH LOVINGLY 19

FINGER POINTING 22

BLAME AND SHAME 24

ENERGY LEAKS 26

WAYS TO AVOID YOUR TRUTH 29

THE BODY NEVER LIES 32

REQUEST RATHER THAN DEMAND 34

IT IS ALL IN THE TONE OF VOICE 36

LEARNING TO LISTEN 38

HOW TO SAY NO 41

DISCERN YOUR HIGHER TRUTH 43

COUNCIL FOR YOUR HIGHER SELF 46

CLEANING HOUSE 52

FINDING YOUR TRUTH 56

REVEAL MORE TRUTH 59

A DAILY PRACTICE
Commit to Yourself

Follow these simple steps daily as a way to instill and strengthen your heartfelt resolve to love yourself. This will help to keep you aligned, transforming and on track, giving you a stable foundation for the rest of your life. As a gift to yourself, please mark the teachings as you read them through and congratulate yourself with each one. See each day as a commitment to take exquisite care of yourself.

- ◊ DAY ONE: WHOSE TRUTH IS IT ANYWAY? 1
- ◊ DAY TWO: BROUGHT TO THE LIGHT 4
- ◊ DAY THREE: BECOMING A TRUTH TELLER 5
- ◊ DAY FOUR: OBSTACLES TO LIVING YOUR TRUTH 8
- ◊ DAY FIVE: SPEAKING YOUR TRUTH INQUIRY 14
- ◊ DAY SIX: SECRETS AND LIES 18
- ◊ DAY SEVEN: SPEAKING THE TRUTH LOVINGLY 19
- ◊ DAY EIGHT: FINGER POINTING 22
- ◊ DAY NINE: BLAME AND SHAME 24
- ◊ DAY TEN: ENERGY LEAKS 26
- ◊ DAY ELEVEN: WAYS TO AVOID YOUR TRUTH 29
- ◊ DAY TWELVE: THE BODY NEVER LIES 32
- ◊ DAY THIRTEEN: REQUEST RATHER THAN DEMAND 34
- ◊ DAY FOURTEEN: IT IS ALL IN THE TONE OF VOICE 36
- ◊ DAY FIFTEEN: LEARNING TO LISTEN 38

- ◊ DAY SIXTEEN: HOW TO SAY NO 41
- ◊ DAY SEVENTEEN: DISCERN YOUR HIGHER TRUTH 43
- ◊ DAY EIGHTEEN: COUNCIL FOR YOUR HIGHER SELF 46
- ◊ DAY NINETEEN: CLEANING HOUSE 52
- ◊ DAY TWENTY: FINDING YOUR TRUTH 56
- ◊ DAY TWENTY-ONE: REVEAL MORE TRUTH 59

A LIFE WORTH LIVING

"Never give from your well.
Always give from your overflow."
~ Rumi

All too often as women, your own needs are denied for the benefit of others as you orchestrate your life through demands and expectations you feel responsible for. Unfortunately, this can leave you without the juice and energy needed to be present fully and to enjoy life. During these readings, you will continually discover more about who you truly are and learn the tools needed to live your most authentic and fulfilling life possible. From this place, you will experience being 'full to overflowing' and all the joy and energy this brings.

As you delve into these teachings, you will explore, laugh, study, share, and freely express who you are. In this sacred space, you will ultimately learn your truth as a woman in order to shine, to embody your own beauty, believe in your own worth, and take exquisite care of yourself. For only in this way can you truly be of service.

During these guidebooks, many of the basic needs of women will be explored such as sleep, nutrition, creativity, movement and time to replenish. A topic has been chosen for each book and a cohesive and practical foundation is laid out to inspire and guide you. This will bring about a new strength and resolve which will allow your needs to become a priority, without letting your outer world dictate otherwise. By the end of our time together, the concept of being confident, loving, serene and passionate will no longer be a distant fantasy. Instead, these and many other extraordinary qualities that you naturally embody as a woman will flow with ease, grace and love.

With life's demands so high, it has become imperative that your needs are first acknowledged, honored and then taken care of. From this vantage point, your relationship with yourself then has the potential to be transformed into one of self-love. The beauty is this in turn creates a life that not only fulfills you and your life's purpose, but also allows everyone touched by your presence to receive this gift.

I look forward to spending this precious time with you.

Welcome to A Woman's Truth.

Sincerely and with love,

FINDING YOUR TRUE VOICE

*"Three things cannot be long hidden.
The sun, the moon, and the truth."*
~ Buddha

In a world where women have been suppressed for centuries, finding your true voice, let alone speaking it, can be both daunting and challenging. Many factors such as society, ancestry, culture and your own personal experiences all lend a hand as to whether it feels safe to speak up, to say no or to actually express who you truly are.

Whose Truth Is It Anyway?

However, life is certainly on an upward curve for women in our culture. Nowadays, women can vote, work, be financially independent, live and even parent alone. The heartbreaking reminder is that in some cultures, women are still being circumcised, their feet bound and are seen as objects or property. Yet, even in today's western world where equality has been fought for and won, you still see women in high-pointed heals, wearing such tight skirts that if they had to run for their lives, basically the would die! Unfortunately, the belief that sexuality is one of a woman's greatest commodities is still rife in our culture.

As a woman, your survival instincts still believe you are at the mercy of your physical limitations. For example, research has shown that a woman of equal height to a man will naturally have less strength and muscle mass. If you look back through the evolution of the human species, when a woman is pregnant, nursing or caring for children, it is clear she is more vulnerable and will need protection. This primal belief can still destroy the rise of a woman's power and voice. Depending on the circumstances that you have chosen for yourself, you might well be reliant on another for your survival needs, such as food, shelter or money.

*Let go of any judgment.
Everyone is dependent on someone.*

The reason this is being brought to light is that, if you do count on someone else, it will be more threatening for you to speak your truth, especially, if your perspective goes against the grain of the person that you are dependent on. This can be triggered in relationships with men, women, bosses, parents or any figure you deem as an authority.

The belief that the fewer ripples you cause, the better your chances of being taken care of, is an ancient DNA training which enforces you to be as pleasing as possible to make sure you get what you need to survive. This is a dangerous equation.

To experience this firsthand, you need to take a moment to think of a time when someone needed your help. If you cared for them and you were getting on well, the chances are that if you could give them what they needed, you would say yes. This is especially true if they asked you in an appreciative and undemanding way.

Now take the opposite scenario. Someone has ignored, belittled or pushed you away. They expect a free license to be as moody as deemed possible, yet they feel entitled to demand your help. More than likely, this will leave a bad taste in your mouth and if you answered yes to these demands, it would probably be seeped in resentment. This proves that the more pleasing you are, the more likely you are to get what you want. In the realm of authentically expressing appreciation and gratitude, this works beautifully. Yet if you are contorting yourself and relinquishing your own authenticity and truth, ultimately manipulation is being used and this does not bode well for any parties involved.

The good news is that, a western world woman can do and have it all. This journey has been well trodden by pioneering women throughout the ages. Yet it is vital to remember that even though you know you are independent and capable of taking care of yourself, that no one is an island. Just as you need the sun and air to survive, human beings need one another. Being open to gratefully receiving help and support, yet remaining solid in your own authentic confidence, is a continuous dance between choosing to be vulnerable rather than believing you actually are.

What is being advocated and encouraged here is for you to always remain your authentic self and to speak your truth. If only it were that easy. The whole issue surrounding the truth is made even more complicated because no one can really identify the whole truth anyway.

When a judge is swearing you in, you are asked to:

"Tell the truth, the whole truth, and nothing but the truth."

In reality this may not actually be possible, because the truth is subjective and is born from each individual's life experience. Therefore, it seems the highest aspiration a human being can have is to tell the truth to the best of their abilities.

The following pages will give you a deeper insight into the unconscious patterns that surround women who are in the quagmire of dishonest living. As awareness is brought to these underlying beliefs, transformation will follow.

Awareness is the key to change.

BROUGHT TO THE LIGHT
The terror behind the curtains.

As you unveil your true self, more and more light will stream through.
As you pull back the curtains and lies, your own true radiance pours forth.
As you choose your authentic truth over distorted beliefs, you become the light.
Yet this light in all its radiance and glory also lives within the shadows.

As the vessel of your being fills with light,
It will vehemently shine upon the dark corners,
The broken spaces and the falsehoods.
All that has been banished and hidden from view will be brought to view.
Instead of simply basking in your newfound liberation, the real work begins.

To reveal the hidden places.
To lovingly cajole the fear from the shadows.
To bring them all into the illumination of love and compassion.

No longer shying away from the truth.
Instead embrace the totality, all of who you are into the fold.
It is only arrogance that believes these shadow sides should not exist.
Ultimately this belief will keep the loathing and judgments alive.
It is in the resistance of pushing them away which gives them life.

In humbleness all resides.
All is welcome.

In humility the whole is embraced
And in acceptance,
It all just simply is.

BECOMING A TRUTH TELLER

*Imagine a world where every person spoke their truth
and it was met with attention and respect.
A world where fear of judgment or intimidation did not exist
and you were loved, cherished and accepted
for who you are. What a world!*

The ultimate outcome here is for you to become your own truth teller and to fully love, cherish and accept all of who you are. For this to be accomplished, it is vital that you spend some precious time discerning what your own truth actually is, even in the light of everyone else's opinions. To stand in the light of your own truth is not always easy to do. Throughout this time of living your truth, you will be guided and lead down a path which will first look at of all the obstacles and beliefs collected through heritage, culture and fear to see if they are blocking your journey. You will then receive the tools you need to know your own reality and have the courage and confidence to align with and speak from your authentic self.

"In the past I spent time with a situation that caused many strong emotional reactions in the people around me. At this point, the story is irrelevant, but I felt as though I was being pulled in many different directions. I would be literally tugged away from my own center and it resulted in a feeling of utter confusion and despair. I credit myself with having a good head on my shoulders and a strong sense of clarity. I love this about myself, which made this scenario even more painful and humbling. In hindsight, I am grateful for the lesson.

I am now extremely clear about the experience and will always remember that the answers always lie within me. I can rise above my reactions and emotions, not delete the facts, and I can connect to the inner guide of intuition that resides within us all."
~ Miranda

As you embark on this journey, notice with whom in your life you can be completely honest. This is a gift worth treasuring. When you cultivate and grow this powerful tool of becoming a truth teller, it is vital that you have an array of people in your community with whom you can practice. They do not even have to be close to you. Saying no to a stranger is a potent lesson.

"Over a number of years, when friends or family asked me to house sit for them, I would always say yes, even if it meant adding stress to my day. Then, after a string of unusual and bizarre events, which involved break-ins, animals dying and natural disasters, I decided I no longer wanted to be responsible for this and began to say no. I now have a reputation of one who does not house sit which suits me beautifully." ~ Miranda

People deserve to be able to speak their truth with confidence and know that it will be received with respect. I hope that most of you have at least one amazing, wonderful friend and confidant with whom you can speak this way. This someone is the kind of person you could say anything to and still be loved and accepted for who you are. Everyone needs to vent, complain and whine occasionally. Whether it is your masculine or feminine self, or perhaps even the child, there are aspects to being human that need to be expressed and worked through with a devoted companion.

You may already have different people with whom you can speak about various aspects of your life. You may go to one person about finances, another about relationships, shopping and decorating tips and still another for the major decisions you need to make. The important thing is that this person or these people are those with whom you can really let your hair down and be your genuine self. They are those trusted beings you can cry, cuss and definitely laugh with and you know it is safe to be who you truly are.

Relationships like these can take time to grow and do require patience. They need to be carefully cultivated and tended to and often require some risk taking on your part. To be truly genuine also requires you to be sometimes vulnerable as well. Imagine if everyone waited for the other person to speak their truth first. The mesh of dishonesty would become unbearable and highly stressful.

*Remember, you can always choose to be the pioneer
leading the way by being honest in every area of your life.*

Interestingly, as you get to know and become more accepting of yourself, you will become your own best friend and confidant. Choosing to treat yourself with the same love and respect as you would your best friend will also serve you in understanding and being more compassionate towards others. In life it is important to know whatever you wish from others, you must first cultivate within yourself.

*As above, so below.
As within, so without.*

Be conscious about making intentions and gestures genuinely heartfelt with the people in your life or you will cheat yourself and others of a true experience.

Taking care of your own needs will help you to speak your truth. You will be more aligned with yourself and be clear as to the direction ahead. If you are tired, hungry or need to pee, then these basic survival needs will become your truth!

"You shall know the truth and the truth shall make you free."
~ Jesus

OBSTACLES TO LIVING YOUR TRUTH
which truths will set you free?

Life is full of situations where it is taught that to lie about certain feelings and desires is acceptable. This can be as simple as telling a child not to cry or the impact of being told you are too loud, too shy or even too demanding. Many of these impressions are formed in childhood and are imprinted by society, culture and ultimately reiterated by yourself when you believe you have to lie in order to fit in. Unfortunately, these lessons are carried out throughout the rest of your life unless they are brought to awareness, transformed and addressed.

The following statements will help you to discern your truth. Hopefully, they may well dismantle some basic deep-rooted beliefs, which may be limiting your ability to be fully authentic and thrive.

TAKE SOME TIME WITH EACH STATEMENT:

See where you may have branded yourself with some beliefs from your past and if some of these new principles may resonate with you more in your future.

◈ **The opposite of your truth is someone else's truth.**

In reality, everyone's truth or perspective is different. Next time you are with a good friend, pick an object to look at from different angles and describe what you see. Even though you are both looking at a bowl of fruit, let's say, your friend's description of the kiwi nestled into a bunch of bananas may seem confusing and inaccurate because from your angle there are bananas but you cannot see even a glimmer of a kiwi. You have half a dozen apples and a grapefruit in front of you. Yet neither of you are wrong. Depending on your view and perspective, the same bowl will look different to each of you. However, it is still the same bowl of fruit.

*The beauty of letting go of the perception of having to be right
is that it frees you of judgment, releases antagonism
and replenishes partnership.*

It is a huge effort to always have to prove yourself. Everyone does it, desperately defending their decision as the right one, even if it means manipulating, bullying or lying to get the other to agree. Imagine your world if you stood strong in the light of your own truth and released the idea that everyone else has to agree with you.

For this to be possible, you need to know your own truth, live in your power and be aligned with your own sense of self worth. Ultimately, this is freedom.

◆ **If everyone likes you, authenticity is no longer viable and you are doing something desperately wrong.**

Were you ever told as a little girl to be nice and behave so others would like you, or at least some version of this? This first laid poison is a potent destroyer of self worth and power. See if some of the following statements sound familiar:

'Be nice… Do not tell… People are looking…That is not very feminine… If you can't say anything nice, don't say anything at all.'

*"You may be able to please some of the people all of the time,
and you may be able to please all of the people some of the time,
but you will never be able to please all of the people all of the time."*
~ Abraham Lincoln

The definition of the word nice is 'to be pleasant, attractive, kind, good and generally approved of'. This works well if that is how you are authentically feeling. However, what about the times when someone has disrespected you and is not responding to you being nice. At this point, to bring out your inner bitch or warrior may well be a more appropriate way to let the person know you are not to be undervalued. If you believe that you always have to be nice, you will not allow the aspect of yourself that defends and protects you, to be present and alive. This puts you in jeopardy and reliant on someone else taking care of you - certainly a disempowering situation.

Take a moment to ponder what version of muting your truth may have been said to you.

"As a child, there were two words that were forbidden by my father. One of the words was 'can't', the other was 'nice'. I still thank him for both of these gifts as it has made me who I am today. There is very little I believe I cannot achieve and if someone calls me nice, I am deeply insulted! I have never really cared what people think of me – this has its pros and cons. Yet in my world, nice is the icing and the decoration. What is important is what lies beneath the surface. Is the cake vital, delicious, interesting, one of a kind? I choose in this lifetime to not be judged by my ability to adorn myself and behave properly. Instead I choose to be my authentic self, even if that means most find me a little too much to handle!" ~ Miranda

If you feel you are caught up in the trap of being nice, liked, pretty, attractive or trying to be what you think others want you to be, pause for a moment. Give yourself the gift of living by the following wise words:

"What others think of you is none of your business."

It is actually impossible to get everyone to like you. Just the nature of you being female will annoy some people. Your skin color, culture, politics, religion, job, accent, looks, body, house, income and marriage are all examples of why anyone could dislike you, let alone your personality or sense of humor. Freedom exists when you give up the need to be liked. By choosing to be yourself, you can decide if you enjoy who you are. Your connection with yourself is the ultimate relationship and is always the one to nurture and explore.

In fact, the next time someone does not like you, congratulate yourself! What that means is that you did not try to become someone you thought they would like and instead you remained true to yourself. The good news is that there are plenty of people in this world who will relish your honesty and your authenticity. It will be a breath of fresh air to them. This is a triumph to your own integrity.

"The first love affair is always with the self."
~ Rumi

◆ **The truth might hurt, but a lie will hurt even more.**

It takes a strong resolve to choose to live by your truth rather than succumbing to a lie. The old adage, 'the truth hurts' was probably coined by somebody who did not like what they were hearing. There are times when a truth can feel searing and seem ruthless. Yet, the bottom line is that what is being said is only someone else's perspective and no one has the power or ability to really hurt your feelings unless you allow them to. The amount of hurt you feel depends on how attached you are to believing what the other person has to say. The same issues can arise when somebody disagrees with your perspective.

The truth may hurt, but not half as much as a lie.

If the truth is laid out, at least there is the potential for a new future. With a lie kept intact and being fed, the past remains hidden, resulting in a confused present, and a tainted and distorted path ahead.

◆ **Most lies are born from fear.**

As you discover more of your own truth and choose not to support lies, you may begin to notice people who are steeped in them. These individuals have set up a dynamic in their lives where they cannot truly be themselves, because, if they let go enough, the truth might slip out. With these personalities, you may notice a veneer or reserve and a strong reactive response to deep honest communication.

Know these people are afraid and desperately trying to find a way to protect themselves. It is up to you whether you choose to stay aligned with them and keep them in your life.

◆ **Why revealing a truth can cause an attack from the one lying.**

There are situations when speaking the truth may cause people to feel threatened and become aggressive. Often, when someone thinks their lie is about to be revealed, their defense mechanism is triggered and they start to attack. You may have noticed this in what can be deemed as dirty fighting. When you find yourself in this dynamic, know that the other person is feeling backed into a corner by their own deceptions. The more light you shine on this state of affairs, the more upset they will become.

Know that this response really has nothing to do with you apart from the fact that you are not supporting their reality anymore. The best remedy is to keep speaking your truth and with love and kindness, allowing them to stew in their own juices. As you come from a place of compassion, remain in your own integrity and still speak your truth regardless.

◆ Whether you choose to be truthful or to lie, you still have no control over another person's reaction.

Often what causes people to lie in the first place is fear of an anticipated reaction and the belief that the other person cannot accept the truth.

This fear of the other person's response to the truth can force people to lie consciously, because they believe it to be the lesser of two evils. They do not want to feel the response or face the consequences of the upset person or deal with the emotions that may arise. Most people choose to lie because they want to manipulate the reaction of the unhappy or angry person.

The solution to this predicament is to realize that you have no control over the other person and their reaction to your truth. The double-whammy is that, by choosing to lie, the other person never gets an opportunity to know who you really are.

It takes courage to stand in your own light of truth. It also gives the other person an opportunity to stand in theirs.

"To thine own self be true."
~ Shakespeare

A 'SPEAK YOUR TRUTH' INQUIRY
Finding the courage to live your authentic life.

The expression 'The truth hurts' can, unfortunately, support you in keeping your beliefs and needs to yourself. As you are now acutely aware, it is vital for women to first acknowledge that it is good to have needs and secondly to give themselves permission to voice these needs. Nobody knows you better than you do. Therefore, relinquish the belief that your family, friends or partner should be mind readers and devoutly begin to read you own mind and reveal your own truth. It is quite possible that not speaking the truth will hurt even more.

TAKE YOUR TIME TO PONDER THESE QUESTIONS:

They will help unveil some of the blockages and fears that may well be in the way of speaking your truth.

◆ How does it feel when you do not speak up?

◆ When does it not feel safe to speak your truth?

◆ What are your obstacles to having healthy and honest communication?

- How do you react when other people speak their truth?

- What happens when you disagree with someone else's truth?

- Do you find it hard to deal with confrontation?

- Do you avoid confrontation?

- What emotions arise around confrontation?

- What effect does confrontation have on:
    - Your breath?
    - Your general well-being?
    - Your voice?

- When does it feel appropriate for you to say no?

- How does it feel when you say no?

- How does it feel when you say yes when you mean no?

- How does it feel when others say no to you?

◆ Do you encourage and allow others to speak their truth?

◆ How does it feel when you do speak your truth?

◆ What do you need to speak your truth?

◆ What is your personal code of ethics, morals and values surrounding truths or lies?

*"For the discovery of truth there is no path.
You must enter the unchartered sea."*
~ Krishnamurti

SECRETS AND LIES

A lie begets a lie and it is certainly a tangled web we weave.

Whenever you are made to keep a secret there is an energetic price to pay. Some secrets, such as a surprise birthday party, can have an air of expectancy and excitement to them, but even they can be stressful.

"A client of mine was lovingly having a surprise birthday bash for her husband. The day of the party filled him with relief, as he had decided she must have been having an affair. For weeks while organizing the party, she would leave the house to talk on her cell phone and lie badly about where she had been!" ~ Miranda

Then there are the secrets that can literally eat away at you. If you come from a family that encourages lies and deceit by saying 'Do not tell so and so', you will have grown up in an environment that supports not telling the truth. This then becomes a familiar and normal way of life. Some secrets are so dark and hidden, such as sexual abuse, that they can destroy slowly and literally your life. Remember, if a relationship needs to be kept secret, it is not worthy of your involvement.

why do we lie?

Often the reason is to try to protect yourself or someone else. Therefore, fear can be the instigator. Think about the last time you were forced to hide the truth. Chances are, you were put between a rock and a hard place and this seemed like the only way out. The trouble with a lie is that it pulls you out of your integrity and ethics. You then have to remember the lie and start to live it as though it were your truth.

There may be a time when telling the truth means hurting someone else's feelings or revealing something that will cause discomfort. Yet remember, your truth can always be told lovingly and the price of a lie is higher than the price of any reaction. With honest communication, any situation can be resolved, especially if both parties are willing to contribute honestly. If this is not the case, then know it may be time to stop investing in the dynamics of the relationship.

SPEAKING THE TRUTH LOVINGLY
A kiss, a truth, a kiss.

Have you ever been in a situation where you know you have to speak the truth because you have dodged the bullet long enough and if you do not speak up, chances are the situation will escalate out of control? Yet you know what you have to say may hurt someone's or cause a negative reaction.

RULES FOR THE BEST POSSIBLE OUTCOME:

- **Get yourself out of reaction mode first.**
  This can take time. If you are emotional and hurt by a person or situation and go in with all guns blazing, the chances are that someone will be shot! You never want to meet insanity with insanity. At least one of you in the situation needs to remain calm and centered. You cannot actually control anyone else; if possible, it is best to spend the energy reining yourself in.

- **Spend some precious time releasing the situation.**
  This could be by talking it over with a wise and nonjudgmental third party or writing out your angst on a piece of paper and burning it.

"I recommend writing out your grievance by hand or being extremely careful if you are using your computer. The whole point is to be brutally honest about your emotions and reactions and it is not for anybody else to hear or see what you write. You are writing so that by the time you sit with the person, you have already let off steam and will not be so volatile. I once heard of a scenario where someone wrote on her computer as an email and 'unconsciously' sent it. There may well have been a part of her that wanted the other person to witness her rant, but the damage caused was huge, as you could imagine." ~ Miranda

Another brilliant way to release anger and resentment is by throwing eggs, smashing plates or popping balloons! This can actually be a form of therapy all in itself. The secret is to set it up so you do not have to spend hours cleaning up the mess afterwards. The actual experience of smashing an egg or a plate is a brilliant release for pent up emotion and anger.

"My daughter and I often go up into the mountains with a dozen raw eggs each. We find a secluded spot, with a canyon wall and spend time throwing the eggs as hard as we can. They smack and explode and the feeling of release and accomplishment is amazing. I realize this may sound a bit strange, but it works. I always feel clearer and less burdened and no one is upset, except possibly the egg." ~ Miranda

Popping balloons is another quick and easy way to bring you back to center. As you blow into the balloon, fill it with all the negative emotions you can muster. As you tie the knot, feel as though you are containing them. As you squeeze or stab the balloon with a pin, feel all the emotions release. You can even color co-ordinate with your feelings. Possibilities are red or orange for anger, green for jealousy or heart ache, blue for suppressed emotions, yellow for feeling bullied or disrespected, black or brown for feeling depressed or toxic.

- **Once you are in a calmer, less emotional and more centered place, it is then time to contact the person and ask to talk.**

- **Start by telling the person something you appreciate and admire about them.**
  Obviously, this is why you would have needed to calm down first. Because when you are angry, it is next to impossible to remember what you like about someone. This is the kiss. Make sure it is authentic and heartfelt. If you are still in reaction mode, this will not be possible as you will want to prove yourself right and justified and you will want to show them as guilty and wrong.

- **Lead the conversation with how you feel.**
  By beginning the conversation with 'I' and keeping it in this mode, will help to stop the other person from feeling attacked and defensive. Examples are: 'I feel confused…I wanted to explain to you…I want to let you know how I feel…'

- **Then express the predicament or situation causing you harm or discomfort.**
  This is the truth. You are clearly stating your perspective on the situation. It is up to the other person how they choose to receive the information. Remember, they do not have to agree. In fact, it is quite likely they may not. This is not the point. What is important is that you are speaking up to express your needs. This in itself is empowering. Whether they can give what you need is up to them. By delivering the truth in a loving way, the matter is kept clear, as it is not muddied by emotions, anger, judgment or defensiveness.

- **Lastly end with a non-literal kiss.**
  Thank them or in some way show your appreciation for their time and attention. Repeat what you love or enjoy about them. This will allow you both to leave the situation respectfully, which then gives space for the truth to be digested and the conflict resolved. Once the situation is no longer charged, if appropriate, this could be the time for a real kiss!

FINGER POINTING

*when pointing a finger at someone else,
you are actually pointing three fingers back at yourself.*

Have you ever noticed that when you literally point a finger at someone, your other three fingers are pointing back at you? Next time you are about to ream somebody with blame take a moment to look in the mirror and ask what you are going to accomplish by choosing judgment, rather than self-responsibility. Often the insult you are about to throw, can come back rather like a boomerang, and whack you on the head.

Whenever a confrontation begins with the word 'you' the other person will automatically become defensive because they feel as though they are being attacked.

Another option is to say, "I feel..."

No one can really argue with how you feel, but they will defend a pointing finger, an accusation or an insult. The other side of this coin is when you choose to take on blame that is not yours. This can happen in situations where someone is pointing a finger at you and instead of pausing to discern if you are responsible or not, you automatically take the hit. Ultimately, this will disempower both parties, as it stops the ability to be in partnership with that person. In this situation, you are choosing, consciously or not, to hold the load while allowing the other person to be unaccountable or irresponsible for their part.

"For years, I would take the blame for many a thing that had nothing to do with me. It was as though the dagger was thrown and instead of getting out of the way, I just stood there absorbing the attack and then proceeded to make matters even worse by then stabbing myself with this blade of blame. I realized over time that I could instead visualize pressing a pause button to discern if the blame or insult being thrown was actually my truth. If I decided it was not, I would metaphorically remove myself from the line of fire therefore protecting myself.

If I felt what was being said was a truth that resonated with me, I would choose to transform the dagger into wise words from one of life's teachers and look to see what adjustments I might need to make. Either way, I was no longer feeling as though I was being stabbed." ~ Miranda

Imagine if someone told you that they hated your bright green curly hair. Chances are, you would decide that this person was either a little crazy or had vision problems. Certainly, you would not take it as some deep insult, wound or truth. You would know that this was someone else's reality and that it was probably safer to disengage.

Problems begin when the criticism pushes on one of your buttons or wounds of insecurity. Deep down, at an unconscious level, you believe part of what they are saying. You will often feel this physically in the body. It could be as mild as a nauseous sensation or as strong as being punched in the stomach. Either way, the wind has been knocked out of you as your own power is deflated while you align with their negative impression of you. A triumphant success would be when your own core strength and backbone is strong enough to be not thwarted or dissuaded by another's opinion.

Much of what is being thrown around on a daily basis is just someone else's perspective and is as irrational and unrealistic as the crazy green hair.

Where in your life you are being blamed?

And where you are blaming others?

A person can fail many times, but there is no failure until they begin to blame themselves or somebody else.

BLAME AND SHAME
The two headed monster that came to stay.

Blame and shame can often feel like two old uninvited friends coming to stay. Unfriendly, yet familiar beings, invading your space, dictating your behavior, ruling your life and keeping you deeply embedded in old wounds.

Unfortunately, blame is what keeps shame alive and kicking, and you in the role of victim. This is supported by the simple belief that what happened was your fault. You know the voice in your head, the cold, hard uncaring one that says: You should have, could have, would have …The other side of the coin is when you blame someone else, you no longer feel responsible and therefore no longer have the need to make any changes. Either way you are giving up your power.

In this scenario, instead of letting go of the past and choosing to embody a loving and compassionate approach to whatever you have done, there is a personal and merciless attack to your treasured self. This belittling and deep disrespect would shock even your enemies. Unfortunately, this old tape has been played so often in your head, that it has become a deep-rooted part of your psyche and to try another approach can seem unfathomable.

The next time the two bullies of Shame and Blame join forces to disable you,

Forgive yourself.

For whatever it was that you thought you did or did not do, however outrageous,

Forgive yourself.

Allow your heart to soften and invite in two new friends:

Love and Compassion.

Encourage them to sit down by your side. Invite them in and allow them to absolve you of any past digressions. Let them give you the gift of living in the now, free from the relentless voice that undermines you. You may notice, there is no longer a place for the two-headed monster to sit.

And keep forgiving yourself...

Adyashanti, one of my dear teachers, beautifully states:

*"If you have a strong desire to be perfect,
you probably should not have incarnated as a human being."*

ENERGY LEAKS
Swiss cheese for the soul.

As a woman, you have been ingrained with lessons of how to care for others.

It is in the very fabric of your being and your femininity to love and nurture. Yet, as you fulfill this instinctive and awe inspiring quality, you can also find yourself not only depleted and neglected, but also beginning to lose your own light, your own energy and your own center.

When you are in the mode of giving too much and are feeling out of balance, you are actually leaking your own vitality out into the world. The ideal scenario is to be so full that you are giving from your over flow, rather than from your reserve. Unfortunately when you are leeching from your reserve tank, you are depleting your own energy and there is less possibility of garnering your own light.

Imagine yourself as a vessel, which receives a certain quantity of energy each day. The amount will often depend on the actions of the day or weeks before. Did you meditate? Did you eat well? Did you get enough sleep? On the other hand, were you burning the midnight oil and are now living on fumes? These and many other factors such as stress will have a direct correlation to the caliber and quantity of the vigor you have. This is especially true if you have been hemorrhaging energy for everyone else and not leaving enough for you. How much you have in your energetic bank account dictates how much fuel is available to spend living your life.

The point is to notice where in your life are you literally springing a leak, just as if a boat might take on water and lose its buoyancy.

where in your life are you wasting your energy?

THE FOLLOWING ARE WAYS PRECIOUS LIFE FORCE OR ENERGY CAN BE WASTED:

These leaks can be connected to the past or the future or it may be that you are just giving your energy away. Regardless, they can deplete you and leave you without the juice needed to function optimally.

- **Anytime a thought is obsessed over, energy is leaked into that thought. This leaves less time for you to spend on where you really want to focus.**

   For example, you might be thinking about an embarrassing situation that happened to you yesterday. It plays repeatedly in your mind. You cannot stop thinking about it. You question and blame yourself, reliving the experience a multitude of times. In this moment, you have just created an energy leak. By giving your attention to that incident, you have punctured a hole in your boat and created a funnel of energy that is now spewing out into the world instead of being saved for you. Be aware of this and stop reliving, rehashing and critiquing your life. What is done is done and the past is one area that can never be changed. The beauty is that by changing the present you will transform your future. Instead, choose to forgive yourself or the other person.

Stop the mental flogging!

◆ **If you mind other people's business rather than our own, you can spring a leak!** How often do you find yourself giving advice that has not been asked for? Interestingly this practice is a great deflector for not looking at your own life. Try the opposite for a day. When you wake up, vow to speak only mindfully, especially when it comes to giving others your opinion. Put a little plug in this potential leak and just listen. In many situations, that is what is really needed anyway. Most people have a powerful need to be listened to and loved for who they truly are. Imagine what might be accomplished if everyone minded their own business and consciously funneled these energies into what they really wanted to see manifested in their own lives.

*If you are so busy helping others to speak their truth,
what room or energy does that leave for you to speak your own?*

WAYS TO AVOID YOUR TRUTH

Procrastination can often be an effective diversion of the truth and poignantly reveals what is deemed unimportant.

Human beings are very curious animals. You would think that whatever is deemed important would be first on the 'to do' list, yet many human behaviors can often seem counter intuitive to reducing stress and even the survival of the species.

"I am always astonished by my own behavior. When I have a writing or workshop deadline, you would think I would be all over it, getting organized and not procrastinating. Instead, I find myself tidying up, watering plants and tweaking cushions. You name it. I find it to do. Then it is an almighty rush of adrenalin at the end to pull off being dressed, presentable or the text written." ~ Miranda

It seems in this culture that a whole set of behaviors are rampant, which are distractions to the truth and keep the flow of adrenaline running.

ASK YOURSELF WHICH OF THESE BEHAVIORS MAY BE KEEPING YOU LOCKED IN LIES:

◈ **Choosing to become so busy and overfilling the tapestry of life so that there is no time to know what the truth actually might be.**
Have you ever noticed how filling your life with the mundane will actually limit your ability to transform in areas where growth is vital for well-being?

◈ **Investing in pleasing everyone else and having no space to see what would actually be nourishing or enjoyable for you.**
A generous offer of your time, money or energy to others can often feel nourishing. Yet when this dynamic is out of balance and you are giving too much, it is important to look at the motivating factor behind the impulse. Looking outside of yourself rather than inward can often be used as a diversion and may be damaging.

- **Consuming your life with worry.**
  By being overly concerned for others, stressing over what may happen or what others may think can often dictate your whole existence. Unfortunately, this rarely allows you to be happy or present to the moment and life can pass you by.

- **Trying to conform to the perception of others.**
  You lose who you are by being concerned and adapting to what others might think. In this reality, your priority becomes 'do they like me yet?'

- **Getting so caught in your own denials, that drama becomes the only way to release your emotions and pent up energy.**
  In this scenario, chaos becomes the perfect arena for the truth to surface, however ugly the delivery.

- **Drama can become the ideal deflection when you are afraid a truth may be revealed that you want to keep hidden.**
  The ensuing chaos becomes its own enactment of the drama, absorbing all the energy thus leaving no space for the truth to be revealed. In this distorted case, the mission of diversion is accomplished.

- **Avoiding the truth for so long, that you are not even aware of the denials and the lies that have become acceptable.**
  In life, certain behaviors over time become habits. Unfortunately, these behaviors then are no longer questioned. By becoming conscious of addictive or negating habits will give you the awareness to change them. In the transformation, whatever was hidden below the surface will then be revealed.

- **Being overly loyal can veil the truth.**
  Every quality has a front and back to it. Being loyal can be a wonderful trait. Yet, being too loyal to the point of not speaking up when that person crosses the line can be highly detrimental to you.

- **Choosing to live in fear is a powerful way to support a lie.**
  The fear will justify the situation, whether it is keeping quiet or convincing you that a torturous situation is bearable.

- ◆ **Rationalizing old stories, lies and beliefs that you have been telling yourself, makes them your truth.**
  These stories may support and justify keeping dysfunctional behaviors alive.

Becoming aware of how you may be avoiding your truth will be an ongoing inquiry, until the truth firmly replaces the denials. Where in your life are you avoiding the truth?

THE BODY NEVER LIES

*If we choose to ignore the quiet, wise voice of intuition,
the message will manifest as a thought or an emotion.
If we choose not to pay attention to these thoughts or emotions,
it will become a physical manifestation.
If we choose to not acknowledge the pain in the body,
the message has nowhere else to go.*

One way to find your truth is to listen to what your body is telling you. This could be through a sharp pain, a dull ache, tightness or even an inability to breathe fully. The body can symbolize emotions or thoughts that are being numbed or stuffed down. The beauty of the body is that its response is real. If your shoulders are so tight that you can hardly turn your head, then it might be that your sense of freedom and flexibility is being limited. Maybe the feeling that you are carrying the weight of the world on your shoulders needs be looked at. Ask yourself:

Do you really have to be responsible for all that you have taken on?

What would actually happen if you let go of some of what you feel you should or have to do? Often it is as simple as stopping to discern if what you are trying to accomplish is appropriate or even possible.

*Next time your body hurts, stop and pay attention.
It really is the most extraordinary and truth telling messenger.*

It will be one of the truest reads possible. It will show how you actually are and much cheaper than going to a psychic or therapy! Interestingly, human beings seem to respond to pain in the body much quicker than reacting to thoughts, emotions or spiritual crisis. Yet in an ideal world, it is much simpler and easier to listen to your intuition or your emotions rather than wait for some excruciating pain.

The next time you are in physical pain, take a moment to inquire as to why the body is responding in this particular way. Before you choose to numb the discomfort through your own poison of choice whether it be food, alcohol, media, television, an argument, sex, exercise, medications or drugs, choose to stay conscious long enough to hear the message your body is desperately trying to send you. The suppression of pain may relieve you in the moment, yet if the underlying cause is ignored for too long, the symptoms tend to spread and lodge themselves elsewhere. There is only so much numbing one can do!

Symptoms in the body start with the brain and your thoughts. A stress or a conflict arises and if the brain does not receive a solution soon enough, it stores the reaction in the cells of the body. It tends to correlate somehow to the situation. For example, if you are having a conflict around your boundaries being invaded, often an infection in the bladder or urinary tract will occur. Think of an animal marking its territory.

Whenever a conflict is not fully resolved, it is stored as a cellular memory somewhere in the flesh of the body. Unfortunately, when a similar situation then occurs in life, the old memory is triggered. You may have noticed this when a seemingly benign event causes a massive reaction in you. Yet, if stress is dealt with as it arises, the tension is relieved and the body is no longer used as a storage unit and will not be forced to cause an array of symptoms.

Imagine that the brain has an overflow, just like a bathtub. When this human computer is flooded with stress, it leaks out into the body. Obviously, this is not a good long-term solution, as stress is seen as one of the major causes for many illnesses.

THE QUESTIONS TO ASK HERE ARE:

◆ Are you listening to your body?

◆ What message is your body trying to tell you in this moment?

REQUEST RATHER THAN DEMAND

*Loving acts of kindness toward yourself
make it possible to pass kindness onto others.*

How does it feel when someone comes up to you demanding your attention, your time or your energy?

"Come here... Do this... Give me... Stop... Wait... Be quiet..."

Many of these statements are what most young children are told are inappropriate. They come across as demanding, bossy, precocious and domineering. Yet often, this is the tone used when talking to loved ones, unconsciously demanding what you need without any concept of whether they are in a position to be able to give it to you. A demand tends to take away any feeling of choice. It feels as though you are being ordered and expected to comply, regardless of your opinion, energy levels or situation.

*So why, if being commanded feels so uncomfortable,
is it still so easy to forget and make demands of others?*

The answer is usually because the situation involves stress. There is a sense of urgency and possibly panic that triggers a harsh demand. In this moment, the person demanding is being unconscious because their survival instincts are being activated because of being in adrenal 'fight or flight' mode.

Think about if you were responsible for a young child and it started to run out into the traffic. The chances are you would not politely say, 'Please can you turn around and not run in front of that car?' Instead, you would probably yell at the top of your lungs, 'Stop! Come here! No!' or some such version. This automatic survival response is appropriate in that moment to save a life. When life becomes stressful, it is hard to remain patient and kind, and it is easy to forget that your situation is not necessarily life threatening. The trouble is, as soon as something is perceived as invasive, the body translates this stress as fear. What is strange about living in today's world is that the threat can be as simple as running fifteen minutes late.

A beneficial habit to form is to take some deep breaths and remind yourself that your life is not in danger, even if you miss the beginning of a movie. This choice about whether you request or demand what you need is all about consciousness.

It will be a triumph if the next time you are stressed, you choose to treat the person you need support from in a loving and respectful way. For this to be possible, you will need to be rested, well fed, in a comfortable environment and possibly not on your period! This may seem like a lot to envision. Yet if you are following 'The Foundational Trinity' of honoring your sleep, eating well and moving the body regularly, all things are possible. Then you can lovingly ask someone if they are able to help you. Without self-care, survival mode will easily take over and a demand will seem like the only option. There is a basic difference between a *request* and a *demand*.

A *request* is posed as a question without the expectation that it has to be responded to. Whereas a *demand* leaves no room for the other person to have an opinion or to honor their own needs.

SOME WAYS TO MAKE A REQUEST MIGHT BE:

- "Can you help me?"
- "Do you have any spare time?"
- "Is this a good time to ask you a question?"
- "Would it be possible...?"
- "Would you mind...?"
- "Do you have a moment?"
- "I was wondering if..."

IT IS ALL IN THE TONE OF VOICE

A tone in the voice can give you power or take your power away. It is a tool governed by either consciousness or fear.

Have you ever noticed how the pitch of your voice changes, depending on the situation. At times, it may be higher, like a little girl and other times lower and more commanding.

"For a while now I have been curious about how my voice is shifting. In the past when the phone rang I would pick it up and be shocked by the high-pitched resonance of my hello. It seemed as though certain people only triggered it. What was even more curious was that the tone of my voice has gradually been dropping into a lower register over the last few years. To let out suddenly such a girlish squeal was always surprising to me. The common denominator was that this mainly happened with people I wanted to please those who felt like authority figures to me. They became the receiver of a nine-year-old Miranda. Obviously, in this scenario I felt out of my power. After becoming acutely aware of this, I began to take a breath before I talked to these people and consciously kept my tone low. A strange occurrence happened. I felt stronger and much more powerful. I felt as though I was meeting them as an equal and that my voice confirmed this." ~ Miranda

As you go through your day, start to pay attention to your voice.

If you find that it is getting higher and higher, know that you are letting your younger persona lead the conversation. The problem with this is that a seven-year-old is not the best person to be driving the bus, especially in a confrontational or scary situation.

Reclaim your womanhood, power, place the young one into the backseat she belongs, and invoke your fully functioning mature adult to handle the conflict.

HOW TO CONJURE THE CONSIOUS LOVING ADULT:

◈ Pause for a moment.

◈ Take a few deep breaths.

◈ Consciously lower your voice.

◈ Choose to be in your power.

◈ And then continue…

LEARNING TO LISTEN

Can you hear me?

With life being busy and continuously moving from one moment to the next, it can be a challenge to take the time to really listen. The tendency can be to hear, process and interpret information so quickly that often a vital piece of conversations can be missed, leading to misunderstandings. This lack of heartfelt communication can cause a reaction in either party, and push a button resulting in someone shutting down or even speaking over another person's conversation. This can then lead to hurt feelings, anger or drama.

It seems that listening may have become a forgotten art form. To *listen* truly means to make a conscious effort to hear and to pay attention. Compare this to the basic skill of being able to *hear*. Hearing means to perceive sound, like an ambient noise that may be only partially processed.

Listening is actually a very simple act. It requires you to be present to the person you are having a conversation with, which may take practice. The good news is that all you have to do is really listen. You do not need to fix, guide or advise. By taking your time to truly listen, you can open your heart, allow your senses to be active, trust your intuition and miraculously you will find the communication and relationship with that person can shift tremendously.

When you are calm and in the moment, it will allow others to be present as well. Slowing down your own inner chatter will allow you to be able to listen actively. This will mean over-riding the voice telling you all that you have to do, worrying about the past or future or wanting to share your own experience.

Remember, listening takes practice and is a skill well worth learning.

"It has been mentioned to me that I do not always listen. For a while, it seemed as though I was resistant and chose not to listen when I was told I did not listen! In fact, I prided myself in being such a 'good listener' that I was not even able to acknowledge this criticism. However, as always, a seed was planted. A small nagging voice in my head kept whispering that maybe I was not listening as much as I thought I was. Then one day, as I was hiking up a mountain, talking about a business idea, it all became clear. I had come up with what I thought was a brilliant idea and my patient, loving friend commented that she had mentioned this a few months ago.

Dumbfounded, I stopped because it really felt as though this was my light bulb going off and that it was a new and revolutionary concept. What I realized is that ideas, information and guidance are being offered to me daily. Some are brilliant, some timely and some that I have no space for at that moment. My sense is that sometimes, I literally have no room to log a new idea. My creative, entrepreneurial, visionary well is so full that there is not one spare ounce of space for a new concept. It then seems as though this idea that is being offered bypasses my conscious brain and gets lodged somewhere in my unconscious where it sits and waits until the opportunity or space arises for it to reveal itself. When I think this is my own brain-wave of inspiration, I am not listening!" ~ Miranda

With this in mind, it is imperative for you to fill your own energy well full to overflowing, therefore allowing your creativity to function optimally. There is always space for new ideas, inventions and inspirations.

The beauty is that once a creative spark is brought to manifestation, you can release it and make room in your head because the idea is birthed and becomes a reality. Another way to clear your head is by writing the idea down. This releases it from the rat race of your mind. Having some space in your own head will ultimately give you the ability to really listen.

By practicing the art of listening, you will become more conscious and in turn will receive the gift of having permission to really listen to yourself. This could range from the subtle messages of realizing you are thirsty or tired to the more profound voice, which no longer will allow you to jeopardize your sense of knowing or fulfilling a life-long dream.

"So when you are listening to somebody, completely and attentively,
then you are listening not only to the words,
but also to the feeling of what is being conveyed.
To the whole of it, not just part of it."
~ Krishnamurti

HOW TO SAY no... no... no... no... NO!

Making this little word your best friend.

It is amazing how difficult it is for women to say no. Unfortunately, it has been ingrained into the Female's belief system that the word *no* can only be used as a last resort, when all else has failed. Because of this state of mind, women often end up saying yes to lists of tasks, favors and other obligations. Even though in all honesty, they would much prefer to say no and, in reality, these tasks can steal their time.

So why is it so hard to say this simple little word, 'no'?

The bottom line is a lethal concoction of 'They won't like me anymore' and the fear of disapproval. There is also the 'Wonder Woman Syndrome' in which you believe you must do it all, and guilt becomes a strong motivating factor. This can result in a 'yes' when a 'no' would be more appropriate. Yet, once you choose to prioritize your time, these weeds will no longer have room to grow. If you love and respect yourself, you no longer invest in whether someone else likes you. Instead, you are focusing on how you feel about yourself. In addition, when you choose to recognize and honor your needs, then there is no guilt in the simple response:

"I am sorry, but I won't be able to do that."

There is a strong tendency in women to give reasons why you cannot say yes. Know this is guilt driven and just let it go. Remember, you do not need to explain yourself.

No is a complete sentence!

Another helpful statement is:

"I will need to get back to you on that."

This gives you time to ask yourself if it is appropriate to do whatever is being requested of you and what the price will be. If you are already spinning on caffeine and exhaustion, the answer can simply be a resounding:

DISCERN YOUR HIGHER TRUTH

The past is your teacher.
The present is your creator.
The future is your inspiration.

At any moment, there is always a choice between indulging the senses, emotions and reactions or aligning with a higher purpose and perspective. The challenge is often to recognize if a reaction mode has been triggered before you have a chance to escape to a higher ground.

Have you ever noticed your senses or emotions overriding a decision that in the long run may well have served you better? Food is a wonderful example of this. When you are feeling overwhelmed, stressed and emotional and it is as though you are possessed to eat that tub of ice cream or cookie or whatever your choice of comfort food may be; in that moment, the part of you that knows how you will feel the next day is ignored by the desire to fulfill your senses and to numb whatever feelings may be arising.

Sometimes it is as simple as pausing for a moment or taking a breath. This activates the higher functioning parts of your brain, which relates to the present moment, rather than the survival part of the brain, the amygdala, which is entrenched in the past. Doing this will allow you to ask the following question:

So what is the truth in this moment?

THE TRUTH OF THE LOWER MIND IS TO SUBCONSCIOUSLY INDULGE THE SENSES.

Always giving the desire of the senses what they want is rather like giving into a child. Just because a bar of chocolate or staying up late watching television seems like a brilliant, child-like solution to feeling stressed, lonely or hurt, does not mean that it is actually a good idea. Yet, when it comes to survival instincts, it is imperative to listen as the senses are designed to keep you alive. Therefore, if you are dehydrated, your body's intelligence will let you know you are thirsty. Responding appropriately will elevate you out of survival mode, allowing the psyche to calm down. This is why it is vital to acknowledge and respond to these needs. The beauty is these requirements will naturally be taken care of by honoring 'The Foundational Trinity' of Sleep, Nutrition and Movement.

By giving the body what it really needs to thrive, it will become more balanced and less extreme in its reaction, thus no longer living on the rollercoaster ride of hormones, fluctuating blood sugar levels and mood swings. This in turn will have an impact on the emotions and vice versa. If you are emotionally calm, the body will respond by becoming more relaxed. It is a win-win situation.

Once you are no longer living in fear, space is available, allowing you to become less attached to the survival world and more aligned with the bigger picture. This permits you to glimpse a more elevated view of life. From this perspective of balance, you are much more likely to be able to handle whatever life is throwing at you and not react by wanting to numb or distract yourself. Having the courage to experience what is actually happening will give you the strength and wisdom to discern the next step and the right action for your future. By not being present to the situation, it is difficult to know which direction to turn.

THE TRUTH OF THE HIGHER MIND IS TO ALIGN YOU WITH YOUR PURPOSE.

When you are choosing to live from a higher perspective, it is important to first question which part of you is the decision maker; the lower road or the more elevated path. To choose the higher path it is vital to know what pulls you off center in the first place. As already mentioned, the senses can play a large role, as does the influx of information that barrages the mind continuously.

"After spending a week studying meditation, I had to laugh. The conclusion I came to was that, if left to its own devices, my mind was completely insane. As I sat in stillness and silence, random, bizarre thoughts would arise, which was fine. What was scary was how I would attach to these thoughts and follow them wherever they chose to go, dragging me here, there and everywhere. Back into my storehouse of memories and forward into the unforeseen future. It was like a roller coaster ride that actually never stopped in the present moment." ~ Miranda

Thankfully, there is a light at the end of the tunnel. Part of the mind does have the ability to become the observer of all the reactions of the body, the emotions and the psyche. This observer has the ability either to align with these lower mind commentaries or to choose to connect to the witness of it all and soar high above the ripples and stresses of daily life. This observer, or witness, can watch the amusement park ride of the mind, yet still align with a sense of stillness and quiet that can reveal a much higher level of consciousness and truth. Inside every one of us there is an extremely wise inner guide and teacher. It is the part that knows intimately the purpose and path you are here to tread. It does not get pulled off track by stimulation and addiction. It has a quiet inner strength; it never changes and is always present, even when you are not listening!

The problem is, it is rather like tuning into a radio. If you choose to play the station that is connected to your survival, to your senses, emotions and reactions, the sound will certainly drown out your still, quiet inner voice. This watcher within does not shout or have a hormonal fit. You literally need to choose stillness and quiet to tune in. Yet the beauty is, as soon as you start to listen, this Self-witness will speak to you. Your choice is to take exquisite care of yourself, and to learn the difference between these voices.

COUNCIL FOR YOUR HIGHER SELF

Connecting to your inner teacher and guide.

Just as the Council was used as a means to get to know the masculine and feminine aspects of yourself, this powerful practice can also be highly informative in aligning you with your own inner guidance.

By following these simple steps you will be led down a path that will reveal a place of stillness and quiet. In this space, you will no longer be ruled by random thoughts and memories, emotions, the ego or your reaction to your senses.

First, it is vital to acknowledge every one of these aspects as part of who you are. They all serve a purpose, yet once you move beyond them, it is as though you have entered a realm where you receive the honor and gift of the presence of your Higher Self and intuition.

SIMPLE AND SAFE GUIDELINES TO HOLD SPACE:

- Everyone is allowed time to express their thoughts and feelings.

- No one has to speak.

- One voice is heard at a time and no one is allowed to interrupt another.

- Each holds a sacred space for the other.

- Remain in the present and in a receptive, listening stance.

TO BEGIN THE COUNCIL:

◆ **Allow yourself to sit or lie down comfortably.**
  Make sure you will not be disturbed and that your body can deeply relax.

◆ **Take a few deep breaths.**

◆ **Imagine a blank screen in front of your eyes.**
  This is where the Council format will be revealed to you. Relax and soften the eyes. The harder you try, the less you will see.

◆ **First, call in your senses.**
  ◊ These are the five physical responses in the body:
  ◊ Sight, hearing, touch, smell and taste.
  ◊ They all need to be acknowledged.
  ◊ Do not judge how they show up. Hearing might epitomize itself as a literal ear, or you might get an image of your body with the senses exaggerated.
  ◊ Be open to whatever is conveyed.
  ◊ Know that these senses are a vital part of your physical makeup.

◆ **Take a moment to just watch and observe how your senses behave.**

◆ **What do your senses have to tell you?**

◆ **Thank them for their presence in the Council.**

◈ Now invite in your ego.
This is the aspect of your being that is programmed for survival. It is all about you, your needs, your perception and your world. The ego is vital for the physical body to survive and get what it needs to live. Yet unfortunately, if the ego dominates, there is very little room for love, compassion and being of service. The journey here on this earth plane is about balancing the two aspects of being human and spiritual. The challenge is to rise above the lower levels of the ego and to align with the spiritual part of your being, which has the ability to see everyone connected as a whole. This aligns with the belief that whatever ripple an individual causes does have an impact on the ocean of all of humanity.

◈ What does your ego have to say?

◈ Thank the ego for all that it does to keep you alive.

◈ Now, call in your knowledge bank.
In this lifetime, you have learned a storehouse of information. It may include impressions from other lives. Again, do not judge how this is shown to you.

◈ About what does your knowledge bank want to inform you?

◈ Thank it for its presence.

◈ Now it is time to call in your emotions.
These could show up in an array of different ways. They may be connected to one of your senses or be working independently.

◆ What do your emotions want to reveal to you?

◆ Thank your emotions.

◆ Now call in your thoughts and memories.
These are also a part of your mental body and if you have spent any time in meditation, you will know how provocative and domineering they can be. Their random, outrageous, poignant slide show, if left to its own devices, will overpower and eclipse any aspect of your intuition and inner teacher.

◆ Do not judge your thoughts, memories, or even attempt to change them.

◆ Just become the witness and observe them.

◆ Thank your thoughts and memories for their presence and all that they have to show to you.

◆ At this point, it will become clear that you are not just your senses.

◆ It will also be clear that you are not just your body, your mind, your ego, your knowledge, your emotions or your thoughts or memories.

◆ Throughout this process, there has constantly been a part of you watching your thoughts, observing your emotions, knowing you are more than the body.

◆ **Now bring your consciousness to the part of you that was observing your thoughts.**
Bring your awareness to the aspect of you that was witnessing the wanderings of your mind, your memories, your ego and your senses. Become conscious of this peaceful, unperturbed part of you that sits in stillness and watches your life.

◆ **Call in this aspect of your Higher Self to be present in the Council.**
This part of you can have many names yet know this is your Higher Self, and your inner teacher and guide. It has no agenda other than to serve your higher purpose. It is steeped in a deep love and compassion for you. It is unaffected by the stains on your mind. It does not judge or complain. It already knows all of who you are. It already sees your power, your divinity and your goodness.

Now take a moment to ask your Higher Self:

what is my purpose here on earth?

◆ **Ask the question and wait in silence for the response.**
Know that you are planting a seed for this answer to come. It may be words or an image. The chances are, it will be direct, succinct and simple.

◆ **If you have another question you need help with, ask it now.**

◆ **Take a moment to give deep thanks and gratitude for this knowledge.**
Even if what you received was not what you wanted to hear, still be grateful for the gift of this inner guide. Just as a parent will take care of a child, your Higher Self may give you an answer that your senses, ego or emotions do not necessarily agree with or like.

◆ **Remember, this place of deep inner knowledge is always available to you.**
This well of inner guidance is forever present and at your disposal. All you need to do is show up and be present to the teachings.

- ◆ Thank this inner guide and teacher deeply.

- ◆ Thank yourself for using your precious time and energy to do deep internal inquiries.

- ◆ Set an intention to allow your Higher Self to guide your life gently and clearly.

- ◆ Ask for the strength and courage to listen to and follow this guidance.

- ◆ Slowly deepen your breath and bring your attention back to your body and the room.

- ◆ When you are ready, open your eyes and remember your teacher's words.

- ◆ Observe how this advice does or does not align with the world you have created. Pay attention to the areas where adjustments and change may be needed in order to become who you truly are.

- ◆ It may feel appropriate to write down the wisdom you received from the Council.

"Intuition is a spiritual faculty and does not explain, but simply points the way."
~ Florence Scovel Shinn

CLEANING HOUSE

If a relationship is toxic and harmful, why would you want to keep it in your life?

The following exercise is a powerful tool to explore the caliber of the people you surround yourself with. As you inquire, you will see how some of your family and friends provide love and support, while others drain or diminish you in some way. What can be confusing is if the same person does both! There are three columns of choice and before you begin to write your list take a moment to read the description for each possible category.

The 'Love And Supports Me' Pile

Obviously, the first column is the one to which you need to cultivate and add new people. Spend time with these people. Express your love and gratitude to them. Laugh and have fun together. The chances are, these relationships are a sweet balance of giving and receiving and that is why the connection works.

The 'Neutral People And Acquaintance' Pile

This column is for the people in your life with whom you have a clean and clear exchange, everyone knows their dynamic and place in the relationship and there is very little drama or emotion. Some good examples are Gardeners, Cleaning People, Repair People, The Service Industry, Mechanics, Doctors, and Vets.

The 'Disrespect Me' Pile

Remember, this list has nothing to do with love. Chances are, some of the people in the third column you love deeply and loathe at the same time. Just because you love someone, does not mean you have to have them in your life. Forgiving them does not mean it is appropriate to spend every miserable Christmas with them.

Hate is only love that has been hurt.

Bear in mind that some people may come into your life to teach you something or, you may be teaching them. Go through the list of people and see if you can begin to notice any recurring themes or behaviors. If certain behaviors are repeated repeatedly, it is important to discern what lessons they are providing you. Once you become aware of the lesson and make the necessary adjustments, you will no longer need to be a magnet for that particular flavor of people and others like them. They will no longer need to be a part of your life.

Once the list is complete, the next step is to eliminate or limit your involvement with the people who only show up on the negative pile. The question to ask yourself is why would you invite someone into your life that is not loving and interested in your well-being? This is clearly not an area in which you need to invest.

The predicament is how do you eliminate this person without causing a tidal wave? This may not always be possible. Prepare yourself to handle the situation as lovingly as you can and remember that the other person's reaction is not your responsibility.

Certain people may be very attached to feeding off you.

Think of them as energy vampires. As you unravel these situations, there may well be a massive reaction. Just as you wean a baby, it might cry or throw a fit. Once again, let go of your expectation. The deed can be done with loving kindness. You might choose a conversation, a letter, a card or to distance yourself from this person.

So now, we move onto the double dippers! The 'Love And Disrespect Me' Pile These are the people in your life who are sometimes brilliant. They love you and support you, yet they can turn on a dime and in the next moment disrespect and attack you. This list takes some discerning. With some, a truthful conversation is in order. Be clear about what you need and what you will no longer tolerate.

This can be a hard conversation, yet you will know by the end of it if they are willing to respect your needs or not. If they are open to changing your dynamic, it may well be worth the investment. Yet if the conversation ends up with more attacks and disrespectful behavior, it may be time to move on and to fill your life with more loving relationships.

Remember that the more dependent you are on a person the harder it will be to speak your truth, stand up for yourself and make the necessary changes to pull a relationship from the symbolic toilet. This is where self-care and self-love will be the support and allies desperately needed in order for you to be able to stand strong and alone if necessary.

This decision will not always be an easy one and perhaps will require some soul searching. In addition, you may experience some grief around the loss. Yet choosing to set a clear line in the sand regarding how you will be treated is a sure sign of loving and respecting yourself. This is surely a victory worth winning.

"Sometimes the hardest decision in life is which bridge to cross and which one to burn."

There is an important point to remember when choosing to eliminate or limit your involvement and interaction with someone, particularly if you need to have a final communication. It is vital for you to do whatever is necessary for yourself, so you can remain as calm and nonreactive as possible during the interaction.

This simple statement can be revolutionary and life changing:

"When you can treat me with respect, we can carry on this conversation."

It helps set clear guidelines to let people know what you will or will not tolerate.

"I have had relationships in my life where I have tolerated disrespect. Over time, I became resentful and angry and ultimately there was very little of value left in these exchanges. Yet, as I learned to speak my truth, I chose to be upfront and honest about what is or is not acceptable to me. Amazingly, I have had some miraculous results. I always choose to address the situation when I am in a calm and non-reactive state. I express how I feel and what I need. Whether the other person is willing or able to change is up to them, but some of my most precious relationships today were born from this honest truth telling." ~ Miranda

PLACE ALL THE PEOPLE IN YOUR LIFE ON THE FOLLOWING LIST:

Be brutally honest. It might be extremely hard or painful to put a certain family member or so-called best friend on the 'disrespect me' pile. Yet, until you are honest about a relationship, it cannot change. No one has to see the list and do not try to be nice. It will sabotage the result.

- LOVES YOU
- SUPPORTS YOU
- HAS YOUR BACK
- GIVES TO YOU

- NEUTRAL PEOPLE
- ACQUAINTANCES
- CLEAN EXCHANGES

- DRAINS YOU
- TAKES FROM YOU
- DISRESPECTS YOU
- LIES OR ABUSES YOU IN SOMEWAY

FINDING YOUR TRUTH

*When aligned with truth, the result is power,
balance and integrity. When harboring a lie,
the result is the unconscious support of denial.*

The following are ways for you to know, acknowledge and fulfill what is true for you. At this point in your life, it is no longer about living under someone else's perception and opinion of you. When you find a truth that resonates deep within your soul, know that if you hold strong to this value and cultivate it as part of your being, all else will fall into place. The question to ask continually is:

WHAT DO I KNOW TO BE TRUE?

◆ **Know your truth around 'The Foundational Trinity.'**
These are some of your basic guidelines.

- ◊ How much sleep do I really need?
- ◊ How often do I need to eat?
- ◊ What kinds of foods vitalize me?
- ◊ How often do I need to move my body?

◆ **Find out what makes you happy.**
And do more of it.

◆ **Listen to the body.**
It never lies.

◆ **Do not numb or suppress your emotions.**
Then they get stored up and can cause dis-ease.

◆ **Speak up about what you need.**
If you do not ask or explain yourself, how is anybody to know what you need?
If you do not ask, the answer is already a definite no.

- Lovingly confront rather than retreat when you feel disrespected.

- Choose a loving approach to conflict rather than anger.

- When confronting a situation always begin with 'I…'

- **Become aware of being a chameleon in a situation.**
  Ask why you need to adapt so strongly and whether it is right action for you. Accommodation will often result in relinquishing your power.

- **Become conscious of the people in your life around whom you find it a challenge to be assertive.**
  They are your teachers and once you are able to speak your truth, they will no longer have the power to intimidate you.

OTHER IMPORTANT TRUTHS FOR YOU TO DISCOVER:

Pull from the well of knowledge you have discovered about yourself as you walk this revealing path of inquiry. Once you have discerned the truth, it is then vital for you to honor and carve out the space for this truth to take seed, blossom and bear fruit.

- How often do I need time alone and for how long?

- How often do I need to zone out and take a vacation from my 'To Do' list?

- How often do I need a real vacation?

- How often do I need mindless zone out time?

- How often do I need to nap, meditate or be in nature?

- How much touch and affection do I need?

- How often do I need a really good laugh?

- How often to do I need time to do exactly what I want to do?

- How often do I need a day of no agendas, timelines and puttering around?

- What else do I know to be true?

Know these are your truths to live by.

REVEAL MORE TRUTH

"All truths are easy to understand once they are discovered; the point is to discover them"
~ Galileo Galilei

Much of the following practices are about traveling inward to unravel and reveal your personal truths. There are obviously some universal truths to be lived by, you are born, you will die and everything is in a state of continual flux. Yet, the truths being talked about here are the ones born from your own code of ethics and morals. The vital thing to keep bringing into awareness is whether the truth is being reproduced from an old wound or imprint, or is a part of your authentic self.

This is a continuous journey of self-inquiry. Please give yourself the gift of investing in your 'Truthwork'. The person who will benefit most is you, as you will no longer be living in denial of who you authentically are.

◆ Read through the written words.

◆ Complete the 'Speaking Your Truth' inquiry.

◆ Practice making requests rather than demands.

◆ Speak up about what you need, therefore heightening your chances of actually receiving it.

◆ Complete the 'Cleaning House' exercise.
This may well take some time, as people come in and out of your life and you choose in which column they belong.

◆ Practice saying 'no' at least three times over the next few weeks.

- ◆ Keep living 'The Foundational Trinity' of honoring and respecting your worlds of sleep, nutrition and movement. This will keep you centered and balanced enough to know and live your Higher Truth.

- ◆ Revisit 'The Council for your Higher Self'. This will guide you to your truth.

Remember, living your truth is a high ideal.

Yet, the benefits and energies of doing so will inspire and lift your spirits,

allowing you to truly thrive.

I wish you all the support, love and integrity to live fully and speak your truth.

Miranda

"Truth is immediate, radiant, here now.
It is not that truth has to be discovered; only you have to become aware.
Truth is already here."
~ Osho

ABOUT MIRANDA
A spirited guide and mentor.

Miranda is a passionate and devoted leader. Her loving and wise support will guide you on a transformational journey as her powerful teachings unveil the truth of who you are. Her gift is to offer potent tools, which inspire exquisite and beautiful self-care and empower you to live the fullest and most authentic life possible. As a mentor and guide, Miranda deeply walks her talk and is fearless about her own path of self-discovery, as she weaves the sacred into the mundane.

The simple, yet powerful premise offered by the mystic Rumi is the foundation of Miranda's philosophy and mission:

> *"Never give from the depths of your well, always give from your overflow."*

Miranda gives Council and Guidance for the Mind, Body and Spirit. With a background in Nutrition and Energy work, Miranda is the Creator of 'A Woman's Truth' and 'The Spirit of Energy', an Author, a Workshop and Retreat Leader, a Reiki Master and Yoga and Meditation teacher. Miranda studies under the guidance of her Beloved teachers Rod Stryker and Adyashanti.

To speak with or follow Miranda, please call or visit:

Phone: 626~798~6544
eMail: Info@MirandaJBarrett.com
Website: www.MirandaJBarrett.com
Facebook: Miranda J Barrett
Twitter: MirandaJBarrett

ABOUT HELENA

A visionary artist.

Helena Nelson-Reed is a visionary artist whose primary medium is watercolor. Born in Seattle, Washington, she was raised in Marin County and Napa Valley, California and today lives in Illinois. A largely self-taught artist whose educational emphasis and degree is in psychology, Nelson-Reed's primary focus is exploring the collective consciousness and the portrayal of archetypal imagery in the tradition of Carl Jung and Joseph Campbell. Rendered in luminous watercolor technique often described as ephemeral, Nelson-Reed's paintings are created in extraordinary detail, pushing the medium of watercolor past the usual limits. Her work may be found in private collections, book covers, magazines and cd covers. Nelson-Reed also has a line of jewelry, calendars and greeting cards.

Helena's Mission:

My images can be interpreted many ways, and for some will serve as portal to the mythic landscape. Descriptions providing background about each painting are available by request. Navigating and translating myth into contemporary wisdom is the traditional way of transmitting information though a shamanic and multi-cultural practice.

Myth, fairy, folk and spiritual lore describe divine beings and supernatural life forms arriving unbidden and disguised. In our earthly dimension, mortals often play similar roles in the lives of one another. Destinies and energies collide and interact, visible and invisible forces are at work. The mythic realms are timeless, offering insight and inspiration. While my paintings have a positive energy, many have roots in the shadows of life experience and human psyche; like the lotus blossom rooted in pond mud. For many, life is one challenge followed by the next, like beads on an endless string.

Take heart! Like goddess Inanna, one may navigate the underworld, move through dark places yet return to the realms of light battle scarred but wiser, richer for the experience. Read the ancient tales, the great mythic literature; draw strength, for they are repositories of wisdom.

Visit Helena's website for her art, purchase information and art to wear jewelry:

eMail: HNelsonReed@Gmail.com
Websites: www.HelenaNelsonReed.com
www.etsy.com/shop/HelenaNelsonReed
Blog: www.dancingdovestudio.blogspot.com
Facebook: MorningDove Design By Helena

MIRANDA'S WORLD

*Ways to stay connected
and aligned with your truth.*

BOOKS:

A Woman's Truth
A life truly worth living.

Priceless teachings reveal your transformational
journey ahead. Obstacles to self-care are explored
as clear and loving intentions are conceived.

The Grandeur of Sleep
Permission to rest.

Miraculous benefits are realized as the worlds of sleep,
relaxation and rejuvenation are explored and deeply honored.

Nourishing Nutrition
Reclaim your health and vitality.

Reap the bountiful rewards while eating as nature intended.
Claim your health and vitality with these simple,
yet powerful tools to nourish and heal your body.

Embodying Movement
Ground your whole being.

Restore balance in your life. Discover how to embrace
your whole being through the life-enhancing benefits of body movement.

Body Care
Cherish your body as a temple.

Learn to honor your extraordinary body
as a living temple and listen to the healing messages she whispers.

Feminine Power
Fully access your supreme birthright.

Welcome and reclaim this intrinsic privilege while living
in harmonious balance between the masculine and the feminine.

The Abundance Of Wealth
Receive the gifts of prosperity.

Understand the energy flow of prosperity and weave
the threads of abundance throughout the tapestry of your life.

Find Your Authentic Voice
The courage to express who you truly are.

Your greatest ally is born
when you courageously speak your truth and claim your unique power.

Loving Yourself
A love affair with the self.

As you become highly attuned to your own needs,
allow love to lead the way. Grant yourself permission
to honor and express your heart's truest desires.
Love yourself, no matter what.

Living A Spiritual Life
Ground your divine essence here on earth.

Discover what spirituality means to you, by consciously
living between the two worlds of the sacred and the mundane.

Service As A Way Of Life
Ignite the fire of love to truly be of service.

By utilizing the gems of exquisite self-care
on a daily basis and honoring your truth, your mission of service is born.

The Crowning Glory
Fully Rejoice in Being You.

A celebration overflowing with love,
blessings, grace and gratitude. Stand confident within
your truth as your mind begins to serve your heart.

The Food of Life
The Versatile Vegetable.

More than just a cookbook,
a comprehensive guide for nourishing your life.

Reiki
The Spirit of Energy.

An insightful guidebook full of wisdom
which introduces you to the potent and healing world of Reiki.

CARDS:

Inspiration Cards
A daily Spiritual Practice.

Sixty-Five cards with simple yet inspirational qualities
to live by and an insightful guidebook to lead the way.

CD'S:

The Grandeur of Sleep and Rejuvenating Rest

An ancient healing art of rest and relaxation.

Simple yet profound practices, which alleviate stress and tension allowing your mind, body and spirit to heal, restore and replenish.

TO ORDER PLEASE VISIT:

www.MirandaJBarrett.com
www.Amazon.com

All books are available in printed or eBook form.

TESTIMONIES
to 'A Woman's Truth' teachings.

"Miranda's wise words have touched many lives. Her books are exactly what we need. Through these books, Miranda gently guides us to a place of self-honoring. She gives us the tools to find our power. The lessons make so much sense that we ask 'Why were we not taught this as children?' After finishing the books, I knew exactly how to tap into my own wise woman within. 'A Woman's Truth' is one of the best things a woman can do for herself, to fall in love with herself. Thank you Miranda."

Rene´ ~ Owner Yoga Studio ~ Sierra Madre, CA

"Miranda is a terrific teacher who has an uncanny ability to understand and get to the heart of everyone who has the privilege to read her books. Miranda is a compassionate and caring person who profoundly cares about her work, which shines through in her teachings and writings of 'A Woman's Truth'. It is an honor to know and work with this remarkable and insightful woman."

Kate ~ CHom, H MC ~ Woodland Hills, CA

"Miranda has created a remarkable journey for women. I now treasure myself and have come to see how extremely important it is to take care of myself as a woman."

Valerie ~ Teacher ~ Pasadena, CA

www.ingramcontent.com/pod-product-compliance
Lightning Source LLC
Chambersburg PA
CBHW080524110426
42742CB00017B/3222